## About This Book

**Title:** *Bones*

**Step:** 4

**Word Count:** 203

**Skills in Focus:** Silent e and trigraph tch

**Tricky Words:** human, organs, protects, heart, break, heal, doctor, animal, move, brain

# Ideas For Using This Book

## Before Reading:
- **Comprehension:** Look at the title and cover image together. Ask readers what they know about bones. What new things do they think they might learn in the book?
- **Accuracy:** Practice saying the tricky words listed on page 1.
- **Phonics:** Look at the title and write the word *bones* on a piece of paper. Point to the pattern *o_e* in the word. Explain that the silent *e* makes the vowel before it have a long sound, saying its own name, /o/. Model how to say each sound in the word *bones* slowly in isolation. Then, blend the sounds together smoothly to say the whole word. Offer additional examples from the book, such as *shape*, *spine*, *size*, and *time*. Also introduce readers to the trigraph *tch*. Explain that this trigraph makes the /ch/ sound.

## During Reading:
- Have readers point under each word as they read it.
- **Decoding:** If readers are stuck on a word, help them say each sound and blend the sounds together smoothly. After reading a sentence, point out words with silent *e* or trigraph *tch* as they appear.
- **Comprehension:** Invite readers to talk about new things they are learning about bones while reading. What are they learning that they didn't know before?

## After Reading:
Discuss the book. Some ideas for questions:
- Where are some of the bones in your body? Do you know the names of those bones?
- What do you still wonder about bones?

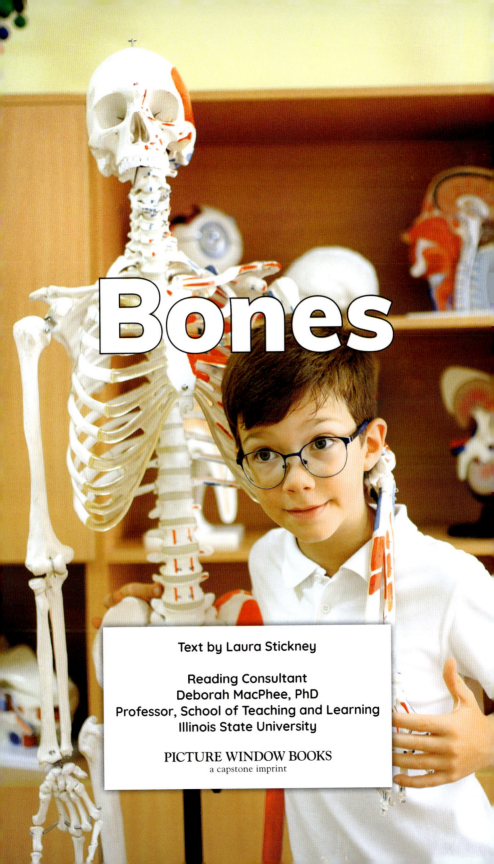

# Bones

Text by Laura Stickney

Reading Consultant
Deborah MacPhee, PhD
Professor, School of Teaching and Learning
Illinois State University

**PICTURE WINDOW BOOKS**
a capstone imprint

## What Are Bones?
The human body is made of bones.

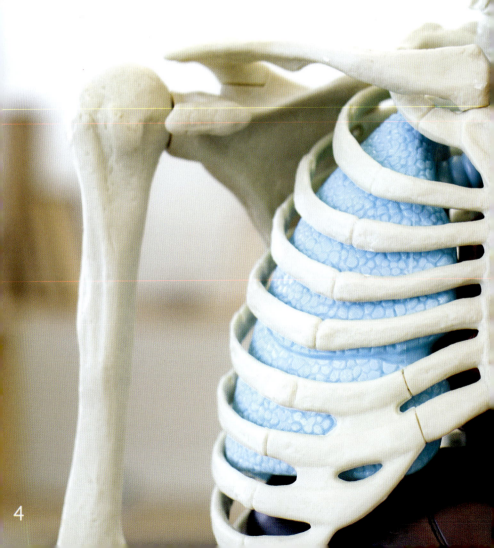

Bones are under your skin. They are hard and white.

Humans have 206 bones.

These bones shape the body.

Bones make your body's soft organs safe.

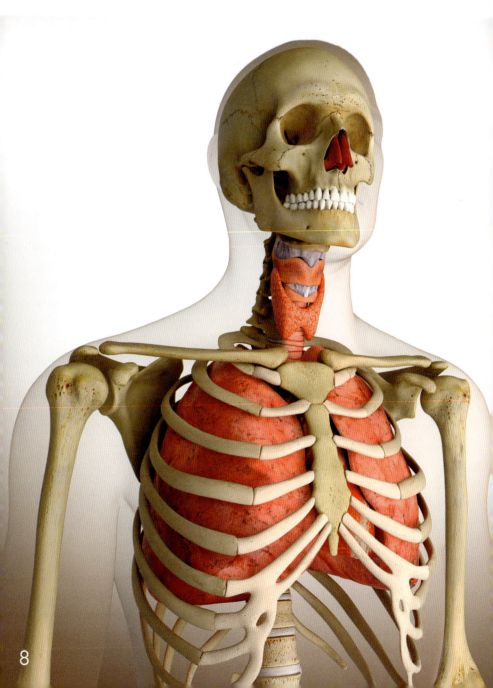

Your rib cage protects your heart and lungs.

The skull is a bone.

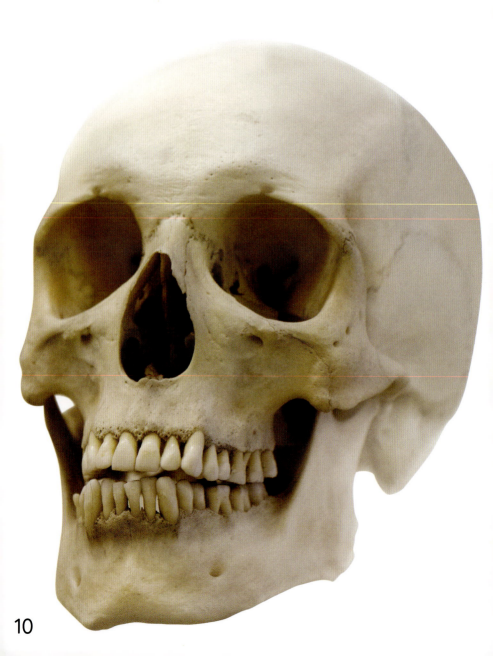

It keeps your brain safe.

Bones help us move. They help us scratch and stretch.

They help us clutch and catch things.

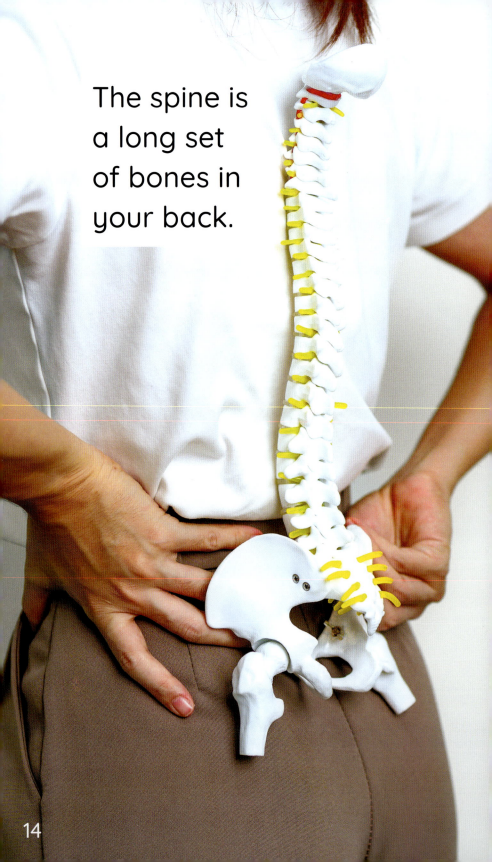

The spine is a long set of bones in your back.

The spine helps you sit and stand.

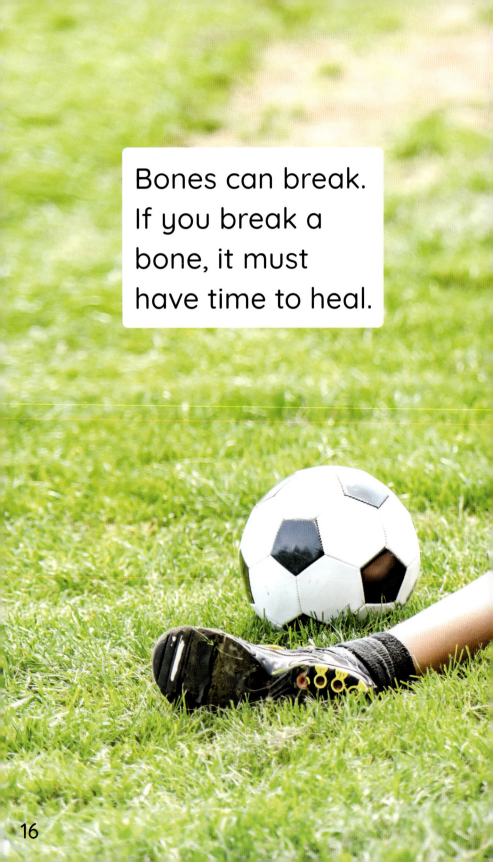

Bones can break. If you break a bone, it must have time to heal.

If you break your arm, a doctor will place a cast on it. This keeps the bone in place.

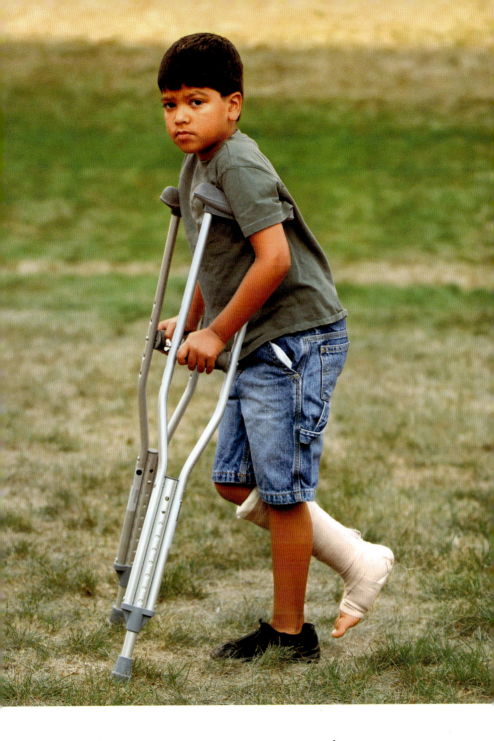

You may use crutches for a broken leg.

# Animal Bones

Animals can have bones.

Some have spines like humans.

Snakes, whales, and bats have spines.

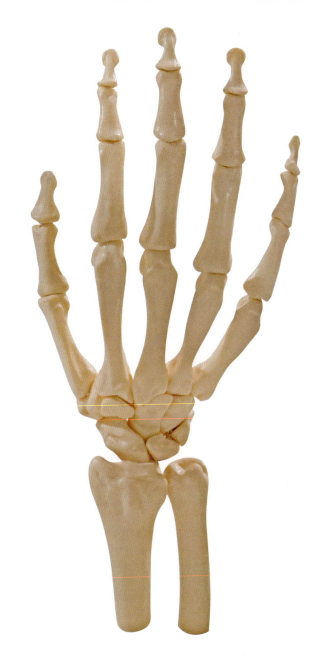

Some bones in your hand match the bones in a whale's fin.

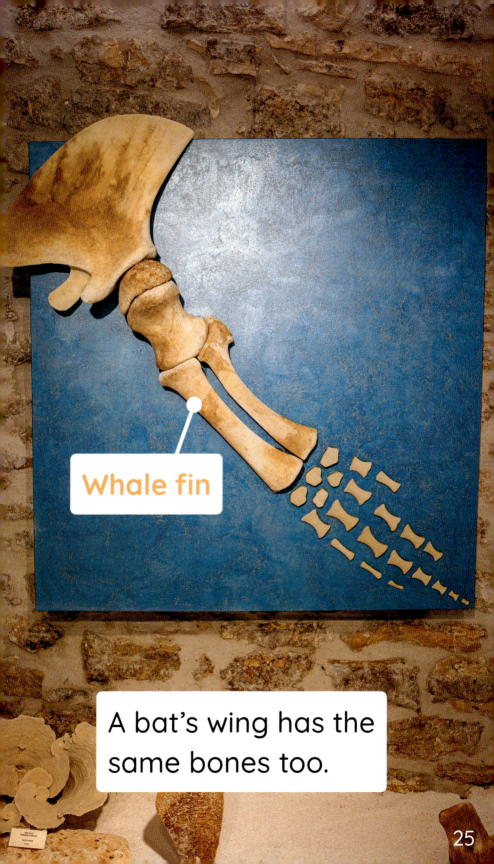

But these bones
are not the same size.

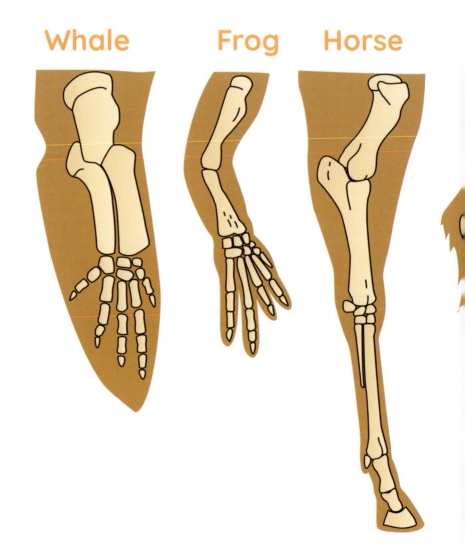

Some bones are big
and thick. Some are small.

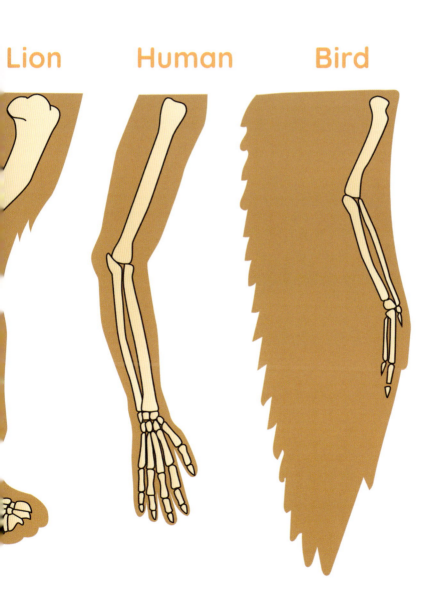

Other animals have no bones. They have no spines.

Bugs and crabs have no spines.

# Bones make us strong!

# More Ideas:

## Phonics Activity

### Writing with Silent *e* and Trigraph *tch*:
Challenge students to write a short story about bones using as many silent *e* words and trigraph *tch* words as they can think of. The story can be as serious or as silly as they'd like!

Suggested words: make, bone, white, shape, cage, safe, place, time, snake, whale, size, spine, catch, clutch, match, scratch, stretch

## Extended Learning Activity

### Studying Bones:
Provide readers with a picture or diagram of a human skeleton. Then ask them to think about the different body parts that each bone belongs to. After studying the picture, ask readers to choose a set of bones. Have readers write a few short sentences about what those bones help the human body do. Challenge students to use silent *e* words and trigraph *tch* words in their sentences.

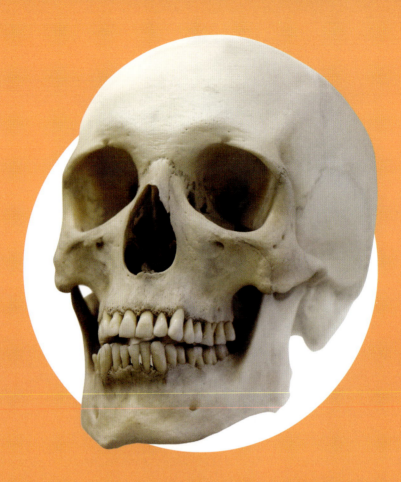

Published by Picture Window Books, an imprint of Capstone
1710 Roe Crest Drive, North Mankato, Minnesota 56003
capstonepub.com

Copyright © 2026 by Capstone.
All rights reserved. No part of this publication may be reproduced in whole or in part, or stored in a retrieval system, or transmitted in any form or by any means, electronic, mechanical, photocopying, recording, or otherwise, without written permission of the publisher.

Library of Congress Cataloging-in-Publication Data is available on the Library of Congress website.

ISBN: 9798875227134 (hardback)
ISBN: 9798875230509 (paperback)
ISBN: 9798875230486 (eBook PDF)

Image Credits: iStock: DrPAS, 10, 32, FatCamera, 18, LSOphoto, 16–17, Zinkevych, 6–7; Shutterstock: A_Lesik, 9, AgriTech, cover, Bangkok Click Studio, 12, Becky Wass, 11, El Cutter, 20–21, glenda, 19, Hryshchyshen Serhii, 3, Jo Panuwat D, 14, Max kegfire, 15, Nadia Candela De Napoli, 28–29, Potapov Alexander, 24, Roman Samborskyi, 1, 30, Sergii Figurnyi, 22–23, SofikoS, 4–5, u3d, 8, Usagi-P, 26–27, Victoria Kurylo, 25, ziggy_mars, 13

Printed and bound in China. 6274